The Truth About
SHARKS

Carol A. Amato
Illustrated by David Wenzel

BARRON'S

Dedication

To Mrs. Busconi's students who helped . . . many thanks.

Text © Copyright 1995 by Carol A. Amato
Illustrations © Copyright 1995 by David Wenzel

All inquiries should be addressed to:
Barron's Educational Series, Inc.
250 Wireless Boulevard
Hauppauge, New York 11788

International Standard Book No. 0-8120-9197-3

Library of Congress Catalog Card No. 95-13378

Library of Congress Cataloging-in-Publication Data

Amato, Carol A.
     Learning the truth about—sharks / Carol A. Amato; illustrated by David Wenzel.
          p.   cm.—(Young readers' series)
     ISBN 0-8120-9197-3
     1. Sharks—Juvenile literature. [1. Sharks.] I. Wenzel, David, 1950– ill. II. Title. III. Series: Amato, Carol A.   Young readers' series.
QL638.9.A56 1995
597'.31—dc20   95-13378
                                                                CIP
                                                                AC

PRINTED IN HONG KONG
5678   9955   987654

Table of Contents

It was a big day for Kate and David. They were going to the aquarium with their class. Some mothers and fathers were coming, too, in order to help. The aquarium was far from their school. They rode in the school bus for a long time. They were all happy when they were there at last!

The aquarium was next to the sea. Their teacher, Mr. Green, said that the sea water was used in the aquarium tanks.

"Boys and girls," said Mr. Green. "We will make five groups. We will meet back here at one o'clock. Billy, Kate, David, and Sue will come with me."

They went inside.

"Why is it so dark?" asked Kate.

"It has to be dark so we can see the animals in the tanks. The tanks are lit up," said Mr. Green. "There are so many things to see! Where shall we start?"

"Look!" said David. "What a big tank! I have never seen a tank *that* big!"

The tank was in the middle of the aquarium. It was three stories high.

Mr. Green said, "That tank is 22 feet (6.7 meters) deep. That's as high as four people who are about 6 feet (1.8 meters) tall! We can walk up and down the ramp to look at the animals inside." The children ran over to the tank.

"Slow down!" Mr. Green called. "Now I know where we will start!"

"There are so many animals in this tank," said Sue. "I don't know where to look first! Oh my! That big turtle looks like it is right next to me!"

"I want to find the sharks! Maybe 'Jaws' is in there!" said Billy.

"Why are those fish all swimming the same way?" asked David.

"Someone is going to help us," said Mr. Green. "We will meet her at the top of the big tank. Don't run!" Mr. Green called to them.

Someone *was* waiting for them.

"Hi, boys and girls! My name is Ms. Woods. I work here at the aquarium. I will show you the aquarium and talk with you today. There are so many animals to see. There is so much to learn. I hope you will ask many questions. We won't have time to see everything today but . . ."

"Oh no!" Kate yelled. "There's someone in the tank. The sharks will eat her!"

"Don't worry," said Ms. Woods. "She's one of our divers. She's feeding the animals. The sharks will not hurt her. All the animals are fed often. We do this so they won't eat one another. Now and then, this may happen, but it does not happen often."

"In the sea, sharks *must* attack and kill so they can eat and live. That is true for all meat-eating animals . . . those who live on the land, in the air and in the sea."

"Ms. Woods, why do sharks attack people?" asked Billy.

"Ms. Woods, why are sharks so mean?" asked Sue.

"Ms. Woods, I hate sharks. Did you see the movies *Jaws*?" asked David.

"Oh my!" said Ms. Woods. "I think we should talk about sharks first!"

Chapter 3

Shark Attack!

"How many of you are afraid of sharks?" asked Ms. Woods. They all put up their hands. Mr. Green put up his hand, too!

"I'm not surprised," she said. "Most people *are* afraid of sharks. If you learn more about them, you may not be as afraid.

"There were three *Jaws* movies about the great white shark. These movies made people even more afraid of sharks. Often, on TV and in some books, only shark *attacks* are talked about. Sharks can and do attack people. They do not attack people as much as you may think. Dogs and bees attack many more people each year! Sharks do not live in the sea just to attack people."

TIGER

BULL

BLUE

GREAT WHITE

"Why *do* they attack, Ms. Woods?" asked Kate.

"We are not sure," she said. "A shark may attack if it's very hungry. If something moves fast or splashes a lot, some kinds of sharks may attack.

"People do not live in the sea. Sharks do. People like to swim in the sea. If someone is swimming in the sea, some sharks may attack. It is hard to know if and when these sharks will attack.

"Most shark attacks happen where it is very hot all year long."

"I thought all sharks were dangerous," said Mr. Green.

"Many people think this," said Ms. Woods. "There are over 350 kinds of sharks. About 30 are dangerous. Most sharks will not harm people. These harmless kinds stay away from people in the sea.

"Sharks attack about 30 people in the whole world each year. Many of these people are hurt but not killed. Most people think that sharks attack much more than this."

HAMMERHEAD

GRAY REEF

THRESHER

WHITETIP REEF

PORT JACKSON

"You and I *would* be afraid of a shark if one was near us in the sea. We would also be afraid of a lion if one was near us on land. Lions, sharks, and other animals that live in the wild may attack people. Many animals may attack people and other animals to protect themselves and their babies. Animals cannot tell if people will hurt them."

LEOPARD

MAKO

"Let's find out more about sharks. Do you have any questions about them so far?" asked Ms. Woods.

"I know sharks are fish. Are they like other fish in the sea?" asked Billy.

"That's a good question, Billy. In some ways they are the same. In other ways they are different. Look at the sharks in the tank. Look at the other fish there. How do they look the same? How do they look different?"

"Many of the fish have more than one color. The sharks here are gray," said Sue.

"Both sharks and the other fish can be big and small," said David.

"The sharks look meaner than the other fish!" said Kate.

"Good 'looking,'" said Ms. Woods. "There are other same and different things that you can't see. Let's look at these pictures of some of the shark's parts. This will help us to understand what they need in order to live in the sea.

"Like other fish, they get their air from the water. They use their gills to do this. You can see the five gill slits on each side of the real shark. Sharks also have two holes above their eyes. Water can go into these holes and pass over the gills. It's another way that the shark can breathe. Bony fish do not have these gill holes."

"Fish have bones. Sharks do not have bones. They have cartilage. That's a big word. Everybody say it . . . CAR-ti-lage."

"Cartilage!" they all said.

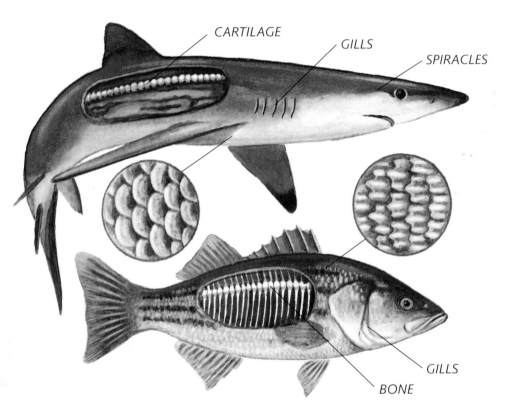

"Cartilage is not hard, like bones. It *is* strong. We have cartilage in our ears and nose. Wiggle the end of your nose. It's made of cartilage. Your bones grow. The shark's cartilage grows.

"Other fish have scales. Sharks do not have scales like other fish. Their scales are shaped like small teeth and are very sharp. This makes their skin very strong."

"The teeth in the shark's mouth look very sharp, too!" said David.

"They are!" said Ms. Woods. "They are sharp to bite and tear food. Sharks do not chew their food. They swallow it whole."

"Once I swallowed my gum whole!" said Sue.

They all laughed!

"The shark has 3 to 15 rows of teeth!" said Ms. Woods. "Some kinds of sharks have more rows than others. When a front tooth is lost, a back one takes its place the next day! How many sets of teeth do *you* get?"

"Just two," said Kate, "and it took a long time for my new front tooth to grow!"

GREAT WHITE SHARK

MAKO SHARK

TIGER SHARK JAW

HUMAN

TIGER SHARK

"Look at these pictures of sharks' teeth and people's teeth. Think about how they are the same and how they are different," said Ms. Woods.

"Are the shark's jaws as big as they looked in the movie?" asked Billy.

"Yes," said Ms. Woods. "The great white has the biggest teeth of all sharks.

"They did not always use a real shark in the movie. The great white is a scary-looking fish. They made a shark that looked even scarier than the real one.

"All shark's jaws are very strong. The jaws must be strong to catch and eat their prey. What does the word 'prey' mean?"

"When you pray for something you want?" asked David.

"Well, you might pray not to be the shark's prey!" said Ms. Woods. "Meat-eating animals all hunt for other animals to eat. The hunted animal is the prey. It is not mean for animals to hunt for and eat their prey. They must hunt so that they can live."

"How fast can a shark swim?" asked Sue.

"A shark can swim as fast as 40 miles per hour," said Ms. Woods. "That's about as fast as some cars go in the city. It can also move slowly—3 to 5 miles per hour. That's slower than you ride your bike!

"It moves like a snake in the sea—from side to side. Its fins help it to swim fast. The two fins near the head look like the wings of a plane. Wings balance the plane. Fins balance the shark."

"These sharks in the tank seem to swim most of the time. Do they ever stay still?" asked Mr. Green.

"Many sharks must swim most of the time," said Ms. Woods. "They must swim to breathe. When they swim, water is pumped over their gills. If these sharks stay still, they will become short of breath. The nurse shark in this tank has muscles around its gills, so it can rest and breathe at the same time.

"We think that sharks do rest. Now we must find out if, when, and how they rest and sleep."

BLACKTIP REEF

"I don't see ears on these sharks. Can a shark hear?" asked Billy.

"The shark can hear *and* see very well," said Ms. Woods. "It has a hole on each side of its head. Its ears are inside these holes.

"The shark and other fish have a sense we don't have. Look at this picture: This sense is on each side of the fish. It lets fish know what prey or enemies are around them."

"The shark has even another sense that other fish do not have. It has many tiny openings or pores around its head. These pores can also sense animals moving in the sea."

"Wow!" said Billy. "They should be called 'super-sharks!'"

"Let's walk down the ramp," said Ms. Woods. "You can see the 'super-sharks' better from there!"

The children hurried to the big tank.

"There's room for everyone!" said Ms. Woods. They each found a spot in front of the tank windows. The diver was feeding one of the sharks. She put the food on the end of a rod in front of it. The shark took it fast!

"What do sharks eat?" asked Sue.

"Most sharks eat fish," said Ms. Woods. "They also eat seals, stingrays, sea turtles, and seagulls! They will eat other sharks, too. Some big sharks eat smaller sharks. Some big sharks try to eat other big sharks. Sharks may eat anything they find! They have found wood, clocks, and many other things inside of some sharks. A shark may only eat once a month.

"The shark can smell blood for many miles. It then follows the blood smell, which may mean prey to eat."

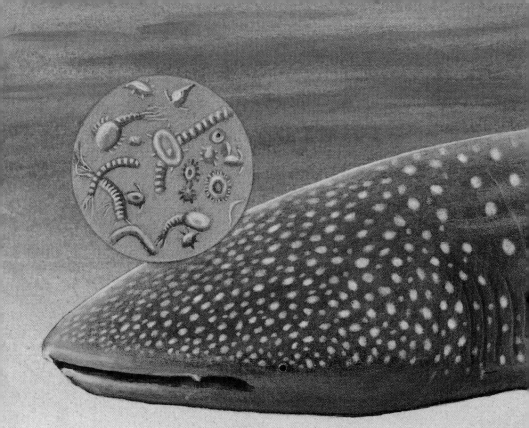

"The biggest sharks eat the smallest food. These sharks are very gentle. One is called the whale shark. It may grow to 45 feet (13.7 meters) or more! It swims slowly with its big mouth open. Tons of water carry food into its jaws. This food is called plankton. It is made up of tiny plants and animals that are carried by the sea. Everyone say this new word . . . PLANK-ton."

"Plankton!" they all said.

"Are they like big strainers?" laughed Sue.

"That is just what they are like!" said Ms. Woods.

"Do sharks live far out at sea?" asked Billy.

"Yes they do," said Ms. Woods. "Most live in the deep sea. Some can live 2 miles deep! Others live in shallow water. Do you know what 'shallow' means?"

"I think it means 'not deep,'" said David.

"That's right," said Ms. Woods. "Most sharks live in the warmer seas of the world. Some live in cold water. A few live near warm rivers and bays.

"Sharks lived in the sea before the time of the dinosaurs. They still live in all of the oceans of the world."

"Do sharks lay eggs like other fish?" asked Mr. Green.

"Sharks can have babies in one of three ways," said Ms. Woods.

"Most shark eggs are hatched inside the mother's body. The sand tiger shark has hundreds of tiny eggs. After they hatch, they must eat each other for food! Only one will live . . . the strongest one of all! When it is born, it swims out into the sea.

"Some mother sharks make an egg case. The mother drops a few egg cases into the sea. About ten months later, the baby shark eats its way out of the case and swims away."

"In some other sharks, the baby is attached to the inside of the mother by a cord. This is almost like the way that people have babies. Only a few babies are born, and they are very big.

"Baby sharks are called 'pups.'

"Like other fish, shark mothers do not take care of their pups. This is not mean. The pups can take care of themselves right away. They have teeth and can swim. It is the way fish and some other kinds of animals were meant to live."

"Ms. Woods, how does a shark take care of itself?" Sue asked.

"The shark must protect itself as soon as it is born. Let's talk about protection," said Ms. Woods.

Chapter 8

The Biggest Enemy

"Sharks are the best hunters in the sea," said Ms. Woods. "They have good protection. How do you think they protect themselves?"

"They have big, sharp teeth!" said David.

"They have 'toothy' skin," said Mr. Green.

"They can swim fast," said Billy.

"They have good senses," said Kate.

"They look mean!" laughed Sue.

"Good thinking!" said Ms. Woods. "Sharks have lived for a long time. Their good protection has helped them."

"How long do sharks live?" asked Mr. Green.

"Each kind of shark may live to a different age. Sharks grow slowly just as people grow slowly. The blue shark lives about 20 years. The thresher and mako sharks live about 40 years. We are still learning about how long sharks live. We think most of them live a long time."

"Do they have any enemies?" asked Kate.

"Big squids may eat them. Killer whales may eat them. The biggest ones do not have many enemies," said Ms. Woods.

"People are the shark's biggest enemies."

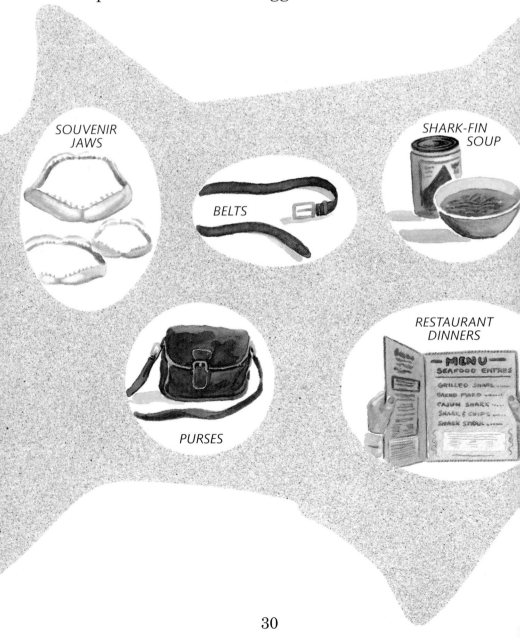

SOUVENIR
JAWS

BELTS

SHARK-FIN
SOUP

PURSES

RESTAURANT
DINNERS

"People use sharkskin to make shoes and belts. They use their teeth for jewelry . . . their fins for soup . . . and other parts of their bodies to make vitamins and even lipstick!"

VITAMINS

JEWELRY

SPORT FISHING

SKIN CARE PRODUCTS

"Many people like to eat shark. Some people like to fish for them. They like to see them jump high in the air when they are caught. Some people think too many sharks are killed for food. The best hunter in the sea is hunted, too!

"Sharks do not get cancer and heart problems. We want to find out why. Sharks may be able to help people."

"We also want to learn more about how smart they are. We would like to know why they are in one place and not another."

"It takes a long time for the big sharks to have pups. The lemon shark takes 15 years to grow up and have pups. It has babies every two years. If it is fished for people's food, it will take a long time for another one to grow up.

"Boys and girls, do you know what the word 'extinct' means?" asked Ms. Woods.

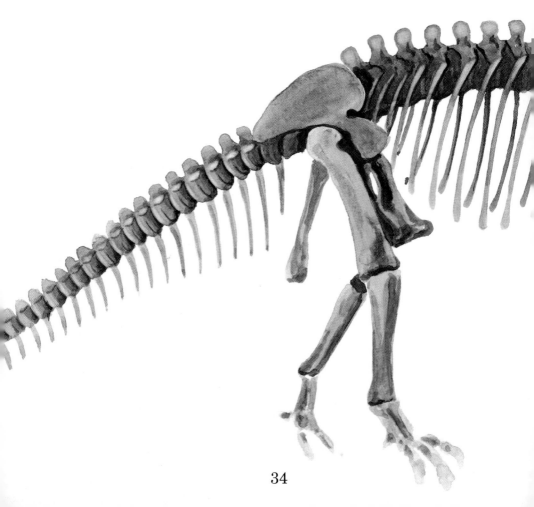

"We learned about the dinosaurs and other animals that became extinct. It means that a plant or animal dies out and there are no more of its kind," said Billy.

"Right, Billy," said Ms. Woods. "Five kinds of sharks have become extinct because of overfishing.

"Let's think about what animals eat, to understand how this can happen."

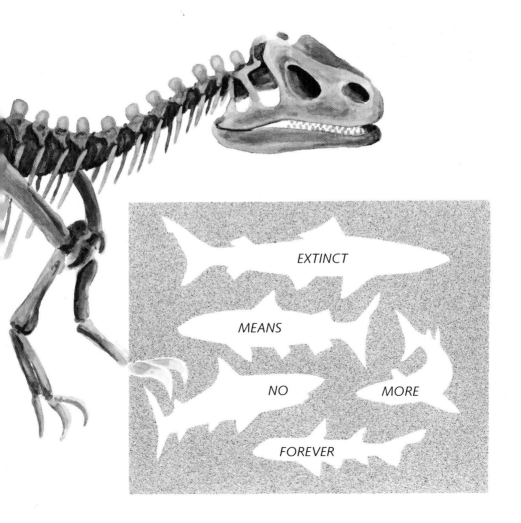

EXTINCT

MEANS

NO MORE

FOREVER

"Some animals eat plants. Some animals eat other animals. Some eat plants *and* animals. They all depend upon each other to live.

"A food chain or web tells about who eats what.

"Let's think about the shark again to see this. Who remembers some of the things a shark eats?"

"Seals!" said Kate.

"Stingrays!" said Billy.

"Fish!" said David.

"Turtles and gulls!" said Sue.

"Each other!" said Mr. Green.

"Good remembering!" said Ms. Woods.

"Now each one of those animals eats other things. A shark may eat smaller fish, the fish may eat mussels, and the mussels may eat plankton. Each one of them helps to keep the balance in the sea.

"The shark is the top hunter in the sea, at the top of the food chain. If we take away this important hunter, a link in the food chain is broken. We must protect the balance of the sea."

"You can see that we must not take away too many sharks, other fish, or sea animals. Many people do not like sharks. They do not care how many are killed. They think that sharks are being mean when they attack people. But to a shark, people are just other animals.

"Sharks were here before people. They belong here as much as we do."

"How can we help to save the sharks?" asked Mr. Green.

"That's a good question. The more we learn about any animal, the more we will care about saving it. When you go back to school, find out about the many kinds of sharks."

"You can write letters to the people who make laws about fishing in the sea. We also need better laws about clean water. Without clean water, many animals will die and may become extinct. Children like you can begin to help even before you are grown up.

"I hope you will come back to the aquarium again! We have so much more to talk about. Please keep asking questions and thinking. Thank you for coming!"

"Thank you, Ms. Woods!" they all said.

On the bus, they all talked about the things they had learned.

"Can we go back to the aquarium soon, Mr. Green?" asked Sue.

"Very soon!" he said. "We all learned so much today, and now we have to get busy. We have so much more to learn and some letters to write!"

Glossary

aquarium (a-QUAR-i-um) a place where people can see animals and plants that live in the water; a tank or container that holds water plants and animals.

attach (at-TACH) to join or connect. In some mother sharks' bodies, a cord is connected to or attached to the baby shark.

attack (at-TACK) a sudden act of force by a person or an animal.

backbone the spine of an animal, which helps to support its body. The backbone of a bony fish is made of bone; the backbone of a shark is made of cartilage. (See *cartilage*.)

balance (BAL-ance) when two forces are equal (the same). Something may have balance when it does not fall off or roll away.

blue shark can be found in oceans all over the world and is very dangerous.

bones found under the skin and muscles of many animals. Bones are hard; they support or hold up the frame (skeleton) of the body.

breathe taking air into the body and letting it out again. People and other land animals breathe through their noses and mouths; sharks and fish have gills that allow them to take air out of the water to breathe.

cancer (CAN-cer) a sickness that can be very serious;

it weakens the cells in the body and causes people and animals to become sick.

cartilage (CAR-ti-lage)   tough tissue in the body that connects the bones of people and other animals. Sharks do not have bones. Cartilage connects the parts of their bodies.

caudal fins (CAU-dal fin)   the tail of fish.

dangerous (DAN-ger-ous)   when something can be harmful.

depend (de-PEND)   to know that someone or something will be there when needed. Animals depend upon each other when they hunt in order to eat and live.

dermal denticles (DER-mal DEN-ti-cles)   the sharp, teethlike scales that cover the body of the shark.

dinosaurs (DIN-o-saurs)   reptiles that lived about 180 million years ago. There were sharks in the earth's seas long before the first animals lived on the land. Their history goes back 400 million years. People have lived on the earth for only 2 million years.

dorsal (DOR-sal) **fin**   fin found on the top side of a fish, in the middle.

egg   the beginning of some kinds of things such as birds, insects, fish, and frogs. Eggs mean new life can begin.

enemy (EN-e-my)   someone who wants or tries to do harm to another. Animals may have enemies because they hunt other animals for food. One is the hunter and the other is the hunted, and they are enemies.

extinct (ex-TINCT)   when a plant or animal dies out and there are no more of its kind. Many animals and plants on the earth have become extinct.

fins   thin, flat parts of a fish used to swim and balance in the water.

food chain or web   tells about who eats what (or whom)! A food chain might begin with a large animal eating a smaller animal and that smaller animal eating an even smaller animal. For example, a shark may eat smaller fish, the fish may eat mussels, the mussels may eat plankton. Some food chains get very complicated and are called food webs because so many animals are part of the web of who eats what (or whom).

gill holes   a pair of holes sharks and rays have also called spiracles (SPIR-a-cles). Water is drawn through the spiracles and passes over the gills.

gills   organs of fish and other water animals that allow them to take air out of the water in order to breathe.

hatch   to come out of an egg. When some fish and birds are born, we say that they have hatched.

jewelry (JEW-el-ry)   rings, bracelets, and necklaces worn by some people.

killer whale   also called orca (OR-ca), a large dolphin that can swallow fish, squid, seals, and sometimes sharks whole. It only kills for food and is gentle with people in aquariums.

lateral line (LAT-er-al line)   a special sense on each side of the fish. It lets the fish know if there is movement (and possibly danger) around it.

lemon (LEM-on) **shark**   a mustard-colored shark. Scientists study the lemon shark because it does well in captivity (that is, after it is captured)!

lipstick (LIP-stick)   used by some people to color the lips. It can be made out of wax, oil, and even shark liver!

mako (MAk-o) **shark**   can be found in warm seas. It is one of the most feared of all sharks because it has razor-sharp teeth that can eat almost any animal.

muscles (MUS-cles)   used to move parts of animal's and people's bodies. People's muscles also help them to lift and carry things.

overfishing   when too many fish are taken from the sea. This means that certain kinds of fish do not have a chance to make more of themselves so that their kind can go on living.

pectoral (pec-TOR-al) **fins**   the two fins near the gill cover.

plankton (PLANK-ton)   small floating or weakly swimming plants and animals that are carried by the waves on currents in the sea. Animals that are filter feeders strain food bits out of the water. The whale shark filters food through 300 bands of tiny teeth and eats tiny plankton and small fishes. Some whales are filter feeders and filter plankton through fine baleen that acts like a strainer.

pores   tiny openings around the shark's head area. Called the ampullae of Lorenzini, these pores can sense electrical signals given off by other sea creatures moving in the sea. The shark then locates this possible prey.

prey   any animal that is hunted or killed for food.

protect (pro-TECT)   to keep from danger.

scales   small pieces of skin that cover fish, lizards, and snakes.

seal   an animal that lives in the sea and swims very well. It has smooth fur and a long body. It makes a sound like a dog barking.

senses   seeing, hearing, smelling, tasting, and touching; ways of feeling.

shallow (SHAL-low)   not deep. There are shallow and deep parts of many different bodies of water such as the sea, ponds, rivers, lakes, and so on.

squid   a sea animal with no backbone. It has a pair of fins, which helps it swim, and ten arms with suckers.

stingray (STING-ray)   a fish that is closely related to sharks. It is a flat animal that has a whiplike tail with a poison spine at its tip.

thresher (THRESH-er) **shark**   can also be found in oceans all over the world. Their tails are nearly as long as the rest of their bodies.

turtle (TUR-tle)   a reptile with a hard shell covering its body. It may live on land or in the water.

vitamin (VIT-a-min)   provide nutrition (what's good for your body). Vitamins are in foods and can also be made by people. Some vitamins are made from the shark's liver.

Dear Parents and Educators:

Welcome to the Young Readers' series!

These learning stories have been created to introduce young children to the study of animals.

Children's earliest exposure to reading is usually through fiction. Stories read aloud invite children into the world of words and imagination. If children are read to frequently, this becomes a highly anticipated form of entertainment. Often that same pleasure is felt when children learn to read on their own. Nonfiction books are also read aloud to children but generally when they are older. However, interest in the "real" world emerges early in life, as soon as children develop a sense of wonder about everything around them.

There are a number of excellent read-aloud natural-science books available. Educators and parents agree that children love nonfiction books about animals. Unfortunately, there are very few that can be read *by* young children. One of the goals of the Young Readers' series is to happily fill that gap!

The Truth About Sharks is one in a series of learning stories designed to appeal to young readers. In the classroom, the series can be incorporated into literature-based or whole-language programs, and would be especially suitable for science theme teaching units. Within planned units, each book may serve as a springboard to immersion techniques that include hands-on activities, field study trips, and additional research and reading. Many of the books are also concerned with the threatened or endangered status of the species studied and the role even young people can play in the preservation plan.

These books can also serve as read-alouds for young children. Weaving information through a story form lends itself easily to reading aloud. Hopefully, this book and others in the series will provide entertainment and wonder for both young readers and listeners.

C.A.

Guidelines for the Young Readers' Series

In the Classroom

One of the goals of this series is to introduce the young child to factual information related to the species being studied. The science terminology used is relevant to the learning process for the young student. In the classroom, you may want to use multi-modality methods to ensure understanding and word recognition. The following suggestions may be helpful:

1. Refer to the pictures when possible for difficult words and discuss how these words can be used in another context.

2. Encourage the children to use word and sentence contextual clues when approaching unknown words. They should be encouraged to use the glossary since it is an important information adjunct to the story.

3. After the children read the story or individual chapter, you may want to involve them in discussions using a variety of questioning techniques:

   a. Questions requiring *recall* ask the children about past experiences, observations, or feelings. (*Have you ever seen movies or TV programs about sharks?*)

   b. *Process* questions help the children to discover relationships by asking them to compare, classify, infer, or explain. (*Do you have to eat every day? Does the shark? Why or why not?*)

   c. *Application* questions ask children to use new information in a hypothetical situation by evaluating, imagining, or predicting. (*In what ways would a lateral line help you?*)

At Home

The above aids can be used if your child is reading independently or aloud. Children will also enjoy hearing this story read aloud to them. You may want to use some of the questioning suggestions above. The story may provoke many questions from your child. Stop and answer the questions. Replying with an honest, "I don't know," provides a wonderful opportunity to head for the library to do some research together!

Have a wonderful time in your shared quest of discovery learning!

Carol A. Amato
Language-Learning Specialist